Exploring
Britain
vol 2: 1970
to modern times

Dr Brian Knapp

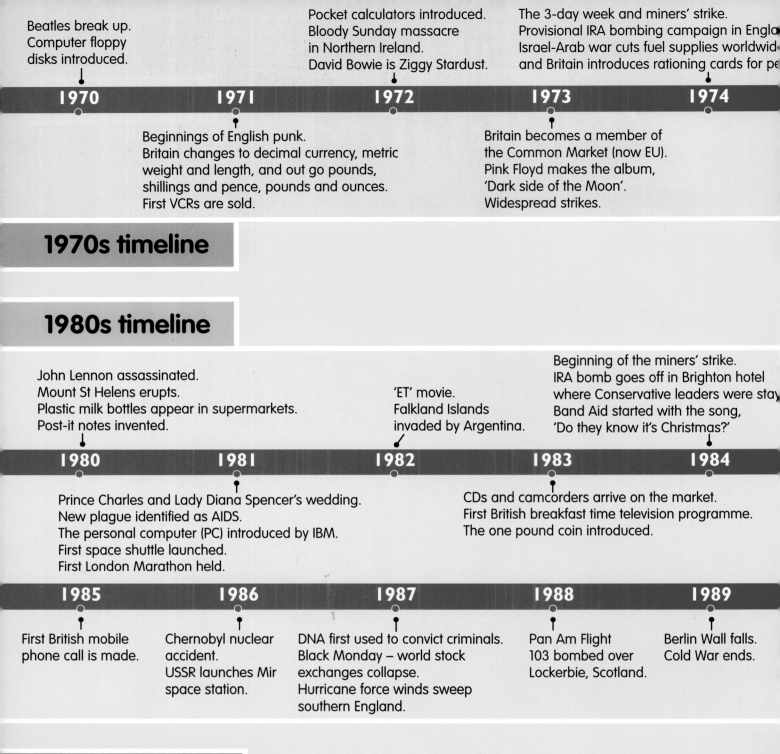

Beatles break up.
Computer floppy
disks introduced.

Pocket calculators introduced.
Bloody Sunday massacre
in Northern Ireland.
David Bowie is Ziggy Stardust.

The 3-day week and miners' strike.
Provisional IRA bombing campaign in Engla
Israel-Arab war cuts fuel supplies worldwid
and Britain introduces rationing cards for pe

1970   1971   1972   1973   1974

Beginnings of English punk.
Britain changes to decimal currency, metric
weight and length, and out go pounds,
shillings and pence, pounds and ounces.
First VCRs are sold.

Britain becomes a member of
the Common Market (now EU).
Pink Floyd makes the album,
'Dark side of the Moon'.
Widespread strikes.

1970s timeline

1980s timeline

John Lennon assassinated.
Mount St Helens erupts.
Plastic milk bottles appear in supermarkets.
Post-it notes invented.

'ET' movie.
Falkland Islands
invaded by Argentina.

Beginning of the miners' strike.
IRA bomb goes off in Brighton hotel
where Conservative leaders were stay
Band Aid started with the song,
'Do they know it's Christmas?'

1980   1981   1982   1983   1984

Prince Charles and Lady Diana Spencer's wedding.
New plague identified as AIDS.
The personal computer (PC) introduced by IBM.
First space shuttle launched.
First London Marathon held.

CDs and camcorders arrive on the market.
First British breakfast time television programme.
The one pound coin introduced.

1985   1986   1987   1988   1989

First British mobile
phone call is made.

Chernobyl nuclear
accident.
USSR launches Mir
space station.

DNA first used to convict criminals.
Black Monday – world stock
exchanges collapse.
Hurricane force winds sweep
southern England.

Pan Am Flight
103 bombed over
Lockerbie, Scotland.

Berlin Wall falls.
Cold War ends.

1990s timeline

Ban on British beef because
of the BSE scare. Hundreds of
thousands of animals were
slaughtered to try to curb it.

The Internet grows
explosively from now
on as the World Wide
Web is created.

Women priests allowed in the Church of Eng
Channel Tunnel opens, connecting Britain ar
France, and Eurostar goes direct to Paris.
The Provisional IRA declares a ceasefire.
National Lottery begins.

1990   1991   1992   1993   1994

The Soviet Union collapses leaving the country we now call Russia.
The Gulf War begins following Iraq's invasion of Kuwait. A coalition
of 30 countries, including the US and Britain went off to fight, but in
the end Saddam Hussein kept control of most of Iraq. It would all
come back to haunt Britain and America in 2003.

Teenager Stephen Lawrence killed 22 April.
London's Bishopsgate bombing 24 April by IRA.
Agreement signed between the UK and Irish
governments on the future of Northern Ireland.

Microsoft founded (which now makes the Windows operating system found on most PCs).

Queen Elizabeth's Silver Jubilee. Elvis Presley found dead. 'Star Wars' film is released in the UK.

Margaret Thatcher first British woman prime minister. Sony introduces the Walkman.

1975   **1976**   **1977**   **1978**   **1979**

Supersonic airliner Concorde 'takes off'. Iceland and Britain fight the cod war over fish supplies in the Atlantic Ocean.

First test-tube baby born' First 'Hitchhiker's guide to the Galaxy' programme goes out on radio. 'Winter of Discontent' with many people on strike.

A Furby toy from the late 1990s.

Contents

Look up the **bold** words in the glossary on page 32 of this book.

Swaminarayan Hindu Temple opens in Neasden and is the largest in Europe. Alison Hargreaves is the first woman to climb Mount Everest without oxygen or sherpas. 13 December – Riots in Brixton.

'Harry Potter and the philosopher's stone' is published. New Labour takes over from the conservatives. Hong Kong returned to China. August 31 – Death of Diana, Princess of Wales. Referendum in Scotland and Wales for devolution.

1995   **1996**   **1997**   **1998**   **1999**

First genetically modified foods sold in the UK. IRA bomb explodes in Manchester city centre. 5 July – Dolly the cloned sheep is born. The Spice Girls release their first record.

Good Friday peace agreement in Northern Ireland. Omagh bombing kills 29 in Northern Ireland. Human Rights Act becomes law.

Minimum wage introduced. The Euro becomes the new European currency. London Eye and Millennium Dome built.

The troubled 70s

In the 1960s, the Prime Minister of the time, Harold Macmillan, told people "You have never had it so good". It was called the 'Swinging 60s'. But by the beginning of the 1970s it all started to go horribly wrong.

People wanted higher wages, but they didn't want to work harder or be more efficient in return. The quality of what was made went down. Our cars, for example, were poorly built, they were unreliable and the bodywork rusted. Buildings – especially skyscraper homes – were put up cheaply and they were not good to live in.

At the same time, people in countries overseas started making things cheaper and better than us. What Britain needed was a 'wake up call', but it did not happen in the 1970s. Instead, the 1970s were a time of **strikes**.

Neither the leaders of the Conservative Party nor the Labour Party got it right. In 1979 it all came to a head under a Labour government in what was called the 'Winter of Discontent'.

Did you know… ?

- In the 1970s the **trade unions** were stronger than the government.
- In 1973 miners went on strike and there was no coal for power stations. Electricity had to be rationed and people could only work for three days a week. There were many power cuts and people had to use candles in their homes at night and when visiting shops.

The 1970s was a time of strikes and when rubbish piled up on the streets.

Q **Why did rubbish pile up on the streets?**

Fashion in the 1970s

The 60s had been a time of 'flower-power' and colour. Some of this was also true in the 1970s. A few people wore leathers and stiff haircuts and called themselves punks. Most men still wore long hair, wide 'kipper' ties, shirts with big collars and flared trousers.

However, a different kind of change was under way. It was because of the new ways people lived. Before the 1970s it was unusual for homes to have central heating, for shops and offices to have air conditioning, or for people to travel everywhere by car.

But during the 1970s these became common. As a result, people didn't have to use clothes to keep warm as much as they had done before. So they were able to use lighter weight clothes (as we do today).

People stopped wearing hats and long overcoats and went for shorter, waist-length duvet coats which were easier to wear in a car.

Trouser suits became all the rage in women's fashion. Platform heeled shoes became common too, for men and women.

Patched jeans

Spacehopper

Miniskirts

6

Bean bag seats

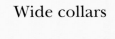

Q **Why did people stop wearing hats and long overcoats?**

Wide collars

Duvet jackets

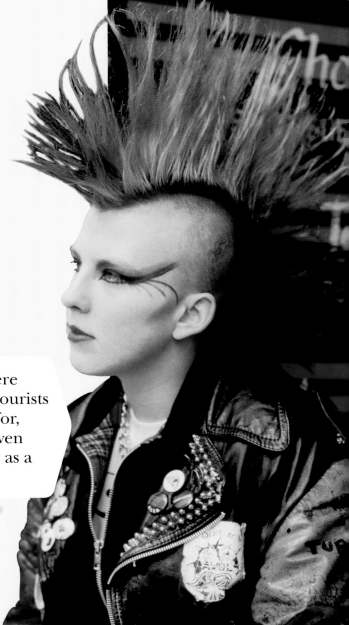

Punk hairstyles were one of the sights tourists came to London for, and punks were even used on postcards as a symbol of Britain.

Platform shoes

Flared trousers

Shopping and cooking

In the 1970s, change in a number of simple things made big changes in how people lived. Two of these were that people now owned more freezers and cars. This may not sound much, but they changed how people shopped in every town and city in the country. Instead of shopping at the corner store each day, more people made a 'weekly shop' to large stores, using their cars to get there, and their freezers to keep food fresh.

There was not enough space for cars to get close to town and city centre shops, so new stores were built on the edges of towns and cities, each with a large car park. The words 'hypermarket' and 'superstore' began to be used.

The 1970s was also the start of '**convenience foods**'. In fact, eating convenience foods was trendy. One of the most famous was the powdered mash potato called Smash.

New fast-food restaurants opened too. The first were Wimpy bars, but by 1974 McDonald's had opened their first store and many more new restaurant chains followed.

Did you know... ?

- "For mash get Smash" was one of the most famous adverts of the 1970s. It used aliens in spaceships laughing at the old-fashioned way Earth people dug up potatoes, peeled them, then cooked and mashed them.

- More overseas holidays than ever were taken and so supermarkets found an ever growing demand for overseas foods, including yoghurt, olive oil and pizzas.

- In the original Wimpy bars you were still served at a table. McDonald's counter service changed that.

- The building of new out-of-town hypermarkets which sold cheaper food in larger amounts was not good news for small shops. The number of grocery stores fell from 150,000 in 1961 to 60,000 in 1981.

Q Why did people start to use hypermarkets?

Did you know… ?

- The comedy shows 'Are You Being Served?', 'Fawlty Towers', 'Porridge', 'Some Mothers Do 'Ave 'Em', 'Rising Damp', 'The Last of the Summer Wine' and 'Monty Python's Flying Circus' are still being repeated today.
- Early computer games used cartridges that plugged into consoles. They were invented in the 1970s, but they became most popular in the 1980s when computers became cheaper.

Over one million skateboards were bought during 1977.

THE WOMBLES ANNUAL 1976
Authorised edition as seen on BBC TV

The Atari 2600 console (above) with joysticks (below) and paddles (above right).

The 'chopper' bike was very popular in the 1970s.

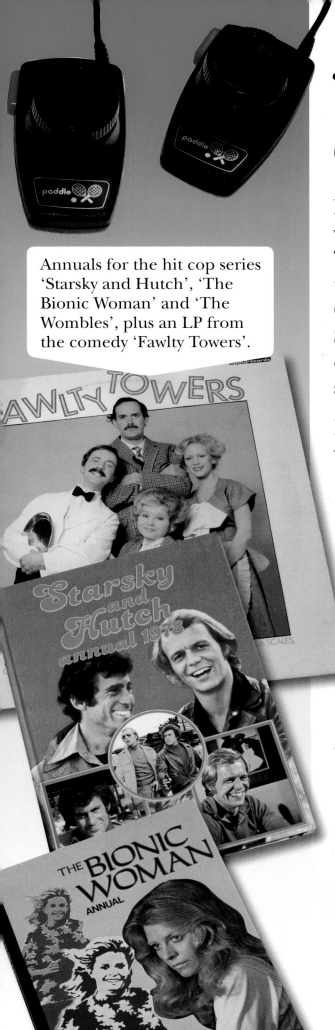

Annuals for the hit cop series 'Starsky and Hutch', 'The Bionic Woman' and 'The Wombles', plus an LP from the comedy 'Fawlty Towers'.

Toys, games and TV

By the 1970s, toy and games makers were using the television to advertise. This meant that they had to have new things to show in the time before Christmas – the biggest selling season. So, in the 1970s, toys and games changed each year. Chopper bikes and skateboards were must-haves.

In the 1970s, computer games were very simple. Anyone with a computer (and there were not many of those) typed in the code and then played the game or used the code that was built into the computer. But in 1977 computer **consoles** that took cartridges were invented. One of the first was the Atari 2600 (shown left, and see also page 19).

Most children were not playing computer games in the 1970s. They were sitting with parents in the living room watching the comedy TV shows. It was during this time that many of the all-time famous family comedy shows were made.

 What do consoles look like today?

The Thatcher years

At the end of 1979, the people of Britain were fed up with strikes and the weak Labour government and they wanted a strong leader. So they elected the first ever woman prime minister. Her name was Margaret Thatcher and she led the Conservative Party. She was to be one of the most famous prime ministers Britain has ever had and she would bring great change during the 1980s.

Margaret Thatcher's first job was to stop strikes and get Britain 'back to work'. But there were overseas problems at the same time. Britain had to win a war in the distant Falkland Islands. The Falkland Islands were invaded by Argentina in April 1982. Britain sent the army, navy and airforce to regain them. They were successful in June. This made Margaret Thatcher very popular.

Margaret Thatcher also worked closely with President Reagan of the USA in the last days of Russian communism. With goodwill from President Gorbachov of the Soviet Union, the 'western countries' agreed to stop being enemies with the Soviet Union, finishing what had been called the '**Cold War**'.

The Falklands War occurred in the early 1980s. Britain had to supply its troops who were fighting on the other side of the world.

The miners fought to keep their jobs and were often in conflict with the police as the police tried to keep protesters and workers apart.

STOP the police STATE

SURRENDER
DUE TODAY
'VE
ON!
FALKLANDS
ARE TAKEN
ORY
Mail
rgentine soldiers
eapons. They are
er Port Stanley
ORY!
Maggie's
sweetest
moment

Did you know… ?

- Margaret Thatcher was known for her strong willpower. When things looked as if they were going wrong, people expected her to change direction (this is called making a U-turn). But she held firm to her decisions and famously said "I have only one thing to say: you turn if you want to; the Lady's not for turning." She was also known as the Iron Lady by the leaders of the Soviet Union.
- Margaret Thatcher was responsible for reducing the power of the unions, famously defeating a year-long illegal strike by some mineworkers.

Q **Which event was Margaret Thatcher most famous fo**

1980s fashion

By the 1980s, Britain was becoming prosperous again. This was the time when working business women took to 'power dressing' – a suit with wide, padded shoulders. The idea was that it showed the world that women were just as able to do well at work as men. It had started in the late 1970s.

Prime Minister Margaret Thatcher and Diana, Princess of Wales both wore 'power suits'. In the early 1980s the style caught on. The successful women in 'Dallas' and other TV soap operas were all power dressers.

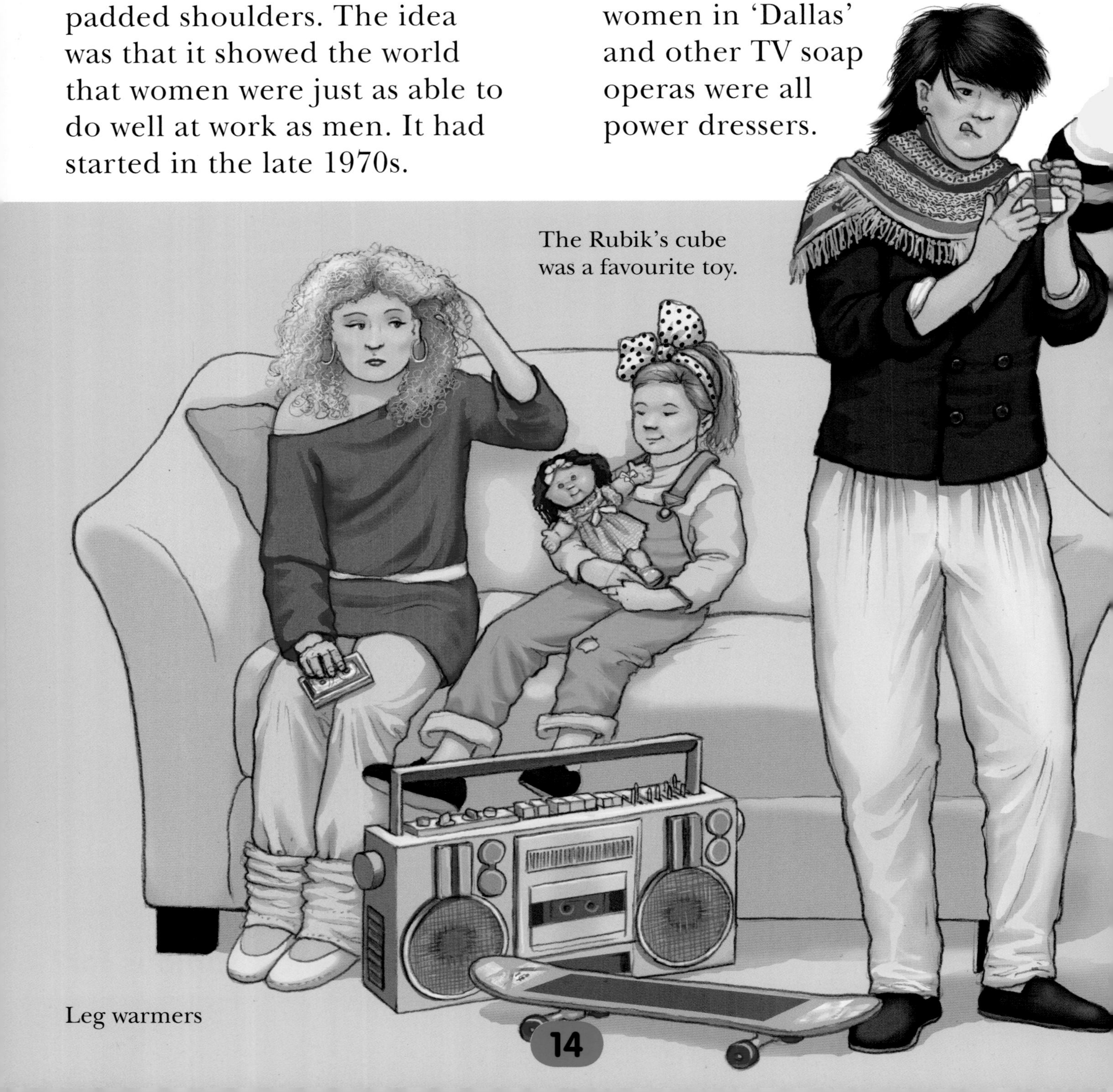

The Rubik's cube was a favourite toy.

Leg warmers

14

The craze accessory for young business people was a Filofax. It was a simple ringbinder diary and organiser that was small enough to fit into a handbag or pocket.

At home dress was becoming more casual and track suits and trainers were worn by many.

Q How did business people dress differently at work from at home?

People wore track suits and other casual wear at home.

Business women wore power suits.

Did you know... ?

- You could get novels that fitted into a Filofax, so you could read them in the train (making sure everyone saw you, of course).
- In the 1980s there was a curious mixture of styles, as women dressed more like men while at work, and men dressed more like slobs when at home.
- This was the first decade where it was trendy to be seen wearing the right brand. You showed how wealthy you were by wearing '**designer clothes**'. In this way, the 1980s was the start of the designer age.
- The 'Magic cube' was invented in 1974, but was renamed 'Rubik's cube' after its inventer in 1980. It was the must-have craze toy. (It may now be the world's best-selling toy, with probable sales of over 300,000,000.)

Television 'soaps'

In the 1980s more and more programmes shown on TV were soap operas. The oldest soap opera (started in 1960) was 'Coronation Street', and for 20 years it ran without competition. Then, in 1985 the BBC launched 'EastEnders' as a south of England rival to north of England 'Coronation Street'.

Up to this time, programmes had been made with small amounts of money, but then British TV started to show American soap operas, which were made like films, with huge amounts of money.

'Dallas' and 'Dynasty' were the most famous. They were about wealthy families and their disastrous lives. The British loved them.

In the 1980s people could record programmes using the new VCRs (video recorders). It also meant that shops could rent out videos. At the same time remote controls were added to TVs and other equipment. All of this started the home cinema way of life.

Did you know... ?

- The words 'soap opera' had been first used in America because the programmes were designed for housewives and mainly showed adverts for soap flakes.
- In 1980 'Dallas' was the most popular TV series in the world.
- Almost without anyone noticing, the 1980s became the first time when satellites were in place around the world, making it possible to show events around the world live.

The cast of 'Dallas'.

Q Why were VCRs and remote controls important?

The first home computers

During the 1980s a ground-breaking event happened: the personal computer (PC) was made affordable. There were computers before this, but they were designed for offices, not for people to use on their own, and certainly not to use at home. They were also expensive.

What changed was that computer makers discovered how to make things work with a mouse, so you could point and click and something would happen. Before that computers could only be operated by keyboards.

Apple Computer was probably the best known personal computer of this age, with its ground-breaking Macintosh (introduced in 1984), but other companies introduced personal computers, too. The most successful software was the one called MS-DOS, developed by Microsoft. This eventually became 'Windows'.

 It was a time when there were many computer makers. In Britain, Clive Sinclair and Alan Sugar sold the ZX80 and the Amstrad range of computers.

Commodore 64 went on sale in 1982. As the name suggests, it had 64 KB of memory. It needed to be plugged into a TV. (Note that PCs are not the same as games consoles, page 10. Consoles are only designed to play games.)

Sinclair ZX81 was named after the year of its release (1981). It had just 1 KB of RAM memory built in. There was also a 16 KB RAM pack that plugged into the rear (most computers now have 1 GB of RAM built in (50,000 times more than the ZX81).

Did you know... ?

- In the 1970s people fed computers instructions on punched cards, so they were impossible for home use.
- A computer in the 1980s cost more in real terms than a PC does today, but it was five hundred or more times slower and did very little.
- The ZX80 was the UK's first mass market home computer. It had to be connected to a TV, which was used as a monitor.
- The first computer games were introduced from the mid-1970s to the mid-1980s. The Atari 2600 (see page 11) used a console, two joystick controllers, a pair of paddle controllers, and a cartridge game such as Combat and Pac-Man.
- In 1982 the Commodore 64 was introduced. Sales totalled 30 million units, making it the best-selling single personal computer model of all time (models change much more quickly now). 10,000 different kinds of software were made for it.

The Macintosh had 128 K of memory and a self-contained 9 inch screen. It was the first computer to use images, rather than text, and a mouse to make things happen. It was responsible for computers being used for desktop publishing.

Q **What was most important in making computers usable at home?**

Aircraft became larger and more seats were added. Some companies discovered that if they offered a very basic service, they could charge less and get more passengers to fly with them.

Did you know… ?

- There was a dramatic rise in the use of aeroplanes and cruise liners, although few people thought about how it might affect global warming.
- Cheap air travel meant that fresh goods could be sent to Britain from all over the world. As a result, people stopped thinking about foods being 'seasonal' because they could be grown somewhere at any time of the year and then just flown in.

The global village

The 1990s were a time of immense change. In the east of Europe the Soviet Union broke apart and communism faded away.

It was a time when people generally became wealthier. The 'New Labour' party came to power, promising to have less to do with the unions than old Labour had done in the past. But above all, during the 1990s, the world 'shrank' and the words 'global village' were used to talk about how easy it was to get anywhere in the world. There were cheap airline flights and people could fly around Europe on holiday more cheaply than ever before. Cheap flights could even make it worthwhile to shop overseas.

There was also a rapid growth in cruise shipping, and huge liners were built to allow thousands at a time to visit places across the world.

While you might go on holiday to another part of the world, there was less need to go out of your home as TV and Internet shopping started to become important.

A cruise liner leaving New York (right). They were designed to let people travel cheaply around the world. Many kinds of entertainment were offered on board (main picture).

Q What was meant by the words 'global village'?

1990s fashion

In the 90s people began looking more casual when out as well as at home. For young people it was the start of grunge.

At the start of the 1990s people were still wearing slim stone-washed jeans, but a few years later they were wearing relaxed (baggy) hip hop fit or widepants. In many secondary schools, young people wore loose cargo pants and fitness sportswear as a general uniform.

Colours became darker, tie-dye shirts came back in from the hippie days of the 70s, hooded sweat-shirts came in and young boys developed the 'hoodie' look.

At the same time, fashion became easy to see and buy on the Internet, and people all over the world began to dress remarkably alike.

One of the new kinds of knitwear was the arrival of the 'fleece'.

Trainers were part of everyone's wear. They had to be designer trainers to be cool – a clever piece of selling by the makers.

Jeans are very important to grunge. They should be ripped, but not too much, or you will look dumb.

Over and undershirts were common.

Girls' hair was straight and hung down.

Flannel shirts were ripped and drawn on.

Did you know... ?

- Grunge came from a 1960s slang term meaning dirty.
- The term 'couch potato' was first coined in 1976, but it became a reality in the 1990s as TV and computer games, using interactive consoles, became all the rage. Doctors started to worry about the health of young people who gave up real games and even going outdoors in favour of computer games.

Cargo trousers were worn.

Q **What was different about grunge?**

Curry made up a quarter of all frozen convenience meals bought.

Italian pizzas started to become more popular than British fish and chips.

Did you know... ?

- Indian Chicken Tikka Masala was Britain's most popular national restaurant dish.
- More than a quarter of chilled meals were Italian; British meals were less than a fifth.
- Far more food was eaten as snacks, much of it while people were on the move. As a result, many new fast food shops opened, including many famous chains from the USA.

Q **Did everyone eat healthy food in the 1990s?**

At up to 70% cheaper there's no excuse not to get your 5-a-day!

Discount chains appeared, such as Aldi, Netto and Lidl, using large warehouses and selling at rock-bottom prices.

On the move

At the end of the 1990s, an average family spent less of their wages on food than in the 1970s. People were also earning more, so the result was they had more money to spend on other things. By the end of the 1990s an average family spent a sixth of their money on wine, beer and spirits – more than ever before.

Superstores got bigger and bigger, but the number of local convenience stores also grew because they opened long hours. Many of them were a part of petrol stations.

Members of families often ate at separate times, and they wanted to spend less time on cooking. In 1980, the average meal took one hour to prepare. By 1999, it took just 20 minutes (often just the time it took to reheat a ready-meal bought from a shop).

In the 1990s some people started to notice that they were too heavy to be healthy. However, they didn't do too much about it. Many people ate processed food and snacked their way through each year.

Mobile phones and the Internet

During the 1990s two very important events began to change our world. Mobile phones changed from being very large and expensive to being small, cheap and usable. By the end of the 1990s, mobile phones had become so common, there were more mobile phones than people in Britain.

The Internet also became part of many people's lives in the 1990s. Because everyone could join in for little money, vast amounts of information was 'published' on the web for others to see. Wikipedia became the world's encyclopedia.

In the 1990s many fewer people had speedy connections, so the Internet was mainly used for sending emails. (In the 2000s it became fast enough to send music and then videos.) This was the time when people went to Internet cafés to send and receive email.

By the end of the 1990s, cheap **broadband** and computer prices allowed most people to have their own computers at home, so they used Internet cafés mostly only when travelling.

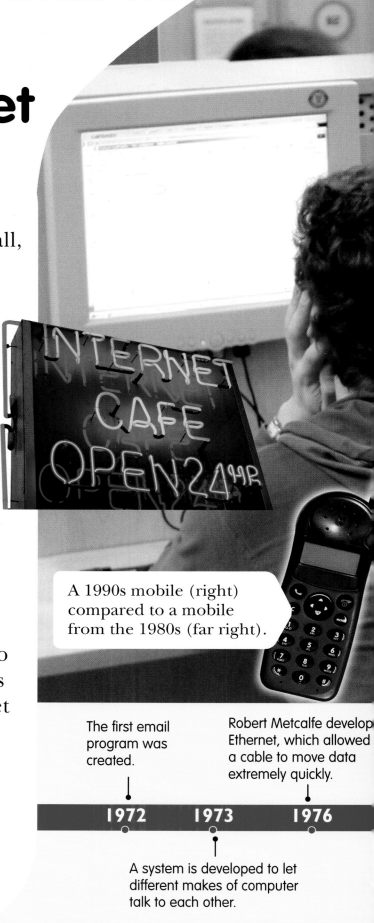

A 1990s mobile (right) compared to a mobile from the 1980s (far right).

The first email program was created.

Robert Metcalfe develop Ethernet, which allowed a cable to move data extremely quickly.

| 1972 | 1973 | 1976 |

A system is developed to let different makes of computer talk to each other.

Early mobile phones were very large – about the size of a brick!

Did you know...?

- The first phone call of a real mobile phone was made in 1978 and the first network was not licensed until 1983.
- The first truly portable phones, using digital signals, were not introduced until 1990.
- About half of all children now have mobile phones. Many children get cheap use of phones through texting.
- In 1994, the idea of a Cybercafé (later renamed Internet café) was invented in London. Here, banks of computers were arranged in a shop (the café) and rented out to people who just came in off the street.

Q Why did the Internet become popular?

World-Wide Web term created. Hosts: 2 million.

Hosts: 7 million.

Hosts: 20 million.

Hosts: 400 million and still growing rapidly.

| 1983 | 1992 | 1994 | 1995 | 1996 | 1997 | 2000 | 2010 |

The University of Wisconsin created Domain Name System (which gives us www.(name)). Hosts: a few thousand.

Pizza Hut offers pizza ordering on its web page. Hosts: 4 million.

Hosts: 15 million.

Hosts: 75 million.

Terrorism

The first part of the new century has been a troubled time. Many people would say that the most important event has been the threat of worldwide terrorism linked to an organisation known as 'Al-Qaeda'.

The moment that changed the world was when two planes were flown into the World Trade Center in New York on 11 September, 2001 (the event now known as 9–11).

The New York's World Trade Center (the Twin Towers) on fire.

Although it occurred in the United States, the suicide bombing had immediate effects on the rest of the world with security checks everywhere. Even so, a disaster hit London on 7 July 2005 when suicide bombers struck the underground and bus systems (now called 7–7).

Efforts to stop new terrorist attacks affect much of our daily lives even today.

People entering and leaving airports and many other kinds of public building now expect body and luggage searches.

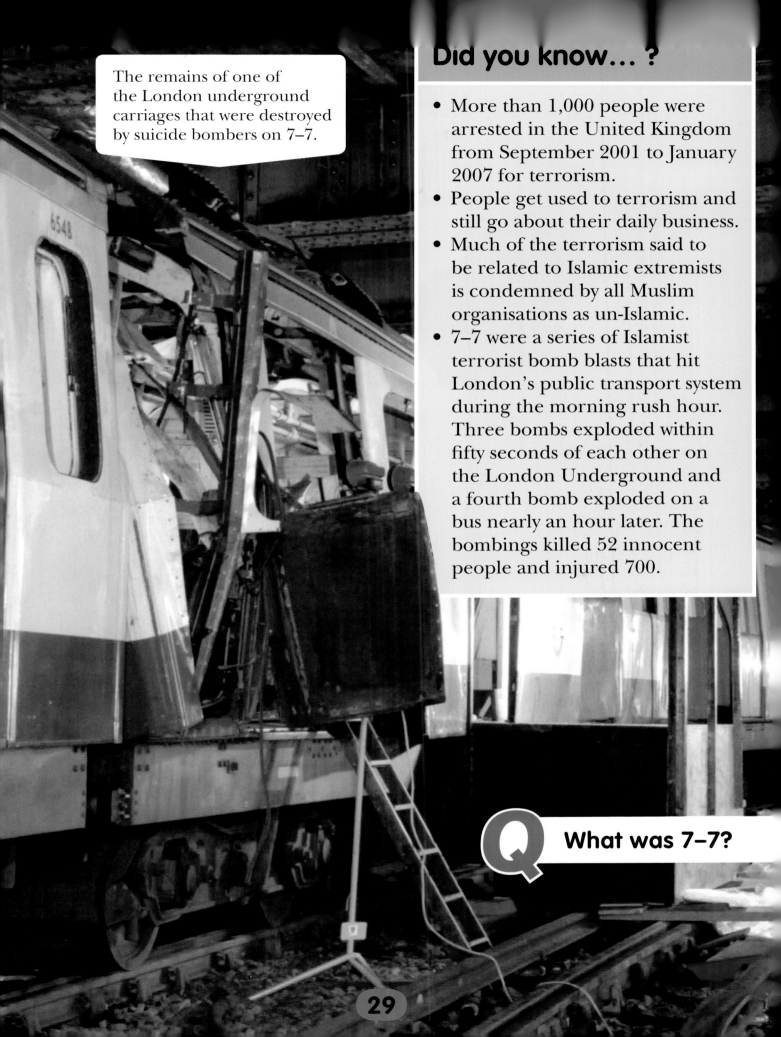

The remains of one of the London underground carriages that were destroyed by suicide bombers on 7–7.

Did you know... ?

- More than 1,000 people were arrested in the United Kingdom from September 2001 to January 2007 for terrorism.
- People get used to terrorism and still go about their daily business.
- Much of the terrorism said to be related to Islamic extremists is condemned by all Muslim organisations as un-Islamic.
- 7–7 were a series of Islamist terrorist bomb blasts that hit London's public transport system during the morning rush hour. Three bombs exploded within fifty seconds of each other on the London Underground and a fourth bomb exploded on a bus nearly an hour later. The bombings killed 52 innocent people and injured 700.

Q What was 7–7?

A new Europe

One of the most important events of the early 21st century was the growth of the European Union (EU). It was founded just after the Second World War to bring countries together who had previously been enemies. It began with six members. The UK became a member in 1973.

In 2004, ten former communist countries of eastern Europe became members of the EU. In 2007 three more countries joined.

This was a very big change because these countries were much poorer than the original EU countries. Some were also home to many tens of millions of people. Their citizens were now allowed to live and work anywhere in the EU they wanted to.

Between 2004 and 2006, about two million people arrived in the UK – many from Poland. At the same time Britain was still taking in immigrants from the rest of the world. As a result of all this **immigration**, the British population reached 60 million in 2006.

Repub of Irela

Portugal

Spain

Did you know… ?

- There are now 27 countries belonging to the EU, with three more waiting to join.
- The arrival of many people from poorer countries meant that they were happy to have low paid jobs.
- Some British people found it hard to get work at a good wage – especially those without skills and qualifications.
- Immigration caused more demand for houses. This made house prices rise.
- 500 million people now live in the EU.

Here are the countries of the European Union. Most of the new EU immigrants to Britain came from north eastern Europe.

Q **What has changed now that the EU has 27 members?**

Finland

Sweden

Estonia

Latvia

Denmark

Lithuania

United Kingdom

Netherlands

Poland

Germany

Belgium

Czech Republic

Luxembourg

Slovakia

France

Austria

Hungary

Slovenia

Romania

Italy

Bulgaria

Greece

Malta

Cyprus

Glossary

BROADBAND A fast means of getting digital signals to move along ordinary telephone wires.

COLD WAR A time, beginning at the end of the 1940s and lasting until the 1980s, when the western countries such as the UK and the USA believed that the Soviet Union was a threat and that real war might soon come if they did not build up stocks of weapons. The Soviet Union believed the UK and USA were a similar threat.

CONSOLE A small computer designed for playing games. Its controls are joysticks and other ways of making things change quickly on a screen.

CONVENIENCE FOOD Food that has been prepared in a factory so that it only needs reheating, not preparing and cooking.

DESIGNER CLOTHES Clothes sold on the reputation of a particular designer. Clothes that sell on a name are also called branded goods.

IMMIGRATION The arrival of people from any country outside the United Kingdom (including the Republic of Ireland and other EU countries).

STRIKE A time when the workers in a company withdraw their labour.

TRADE UNION An organisation which is supposed to look after the working interests of its members.

Index

Curriculum Visions

Curriculum Visions Explorers
This series provides straightforward introductions to key worlds and ideas.

You might also be interested in
Our slightly more detailed book, 'Changing Britain vol 2: 1970 to modern times'. There is a Teacher's Guide to match 'Changing Britain vol 2: 1970 to modern times'. Additional notes in PDF format are also available from the publisher to support 'Exploring Britain vol 2: 1970 to modern times'.
All of these products are suitable for KS2.

Dedicated Web Site
Watch movies, see many more pictures and read much more in detail about post-war Britain at:

www.curriculumvisions.com
(Professional Zone: subscription required)

A CVP Book
Copyright © 2008 Earthscape

The right of Brian Knapp to be identified as the author of this work has been asserted by him in accordance with the Copyright, Designs and Patents Act 1988.

All rights reserved. No part of this publication may be reproduced, stored in a retrieval system, or transmitted in any form or by any means, electronic, mechanical, photocopying, recording or otherwise, without prior permission of the copyright holder.

Author
Brian Knapp, BSc, PhD

Senior Designer
Adele Humphries, BA

Editor
Gillian Gatehouse

Photographs
The Earthscape Picture Library, except *Alamy* pages 4–5; *ShutterStock* pages 10tr, 19t; *TopFoto* pages 6, 8–9 (main), 12–13, 16–17, 18–19 (main), 24–25, 27, 28–29; *www.raleighchopper.info* page 10br.

Illustrations
Mark Stacey

Designed and produced by
Earthscape

Printed in China by
WKT Company Ltd

Exploring Britain vol 2: 1970 to modern times – *Curriculum Visions*
A CIP record for this book is available from the British Library
ISBN 978 1 86214 219 0

This product is manufactured from sustainable managed forests. For every tree cut down at least one more is planted.